DOODLE ANIMALS

Stress Relief Zentangle
Coloring Book For Adults

Illustrated by Maryna Salagub

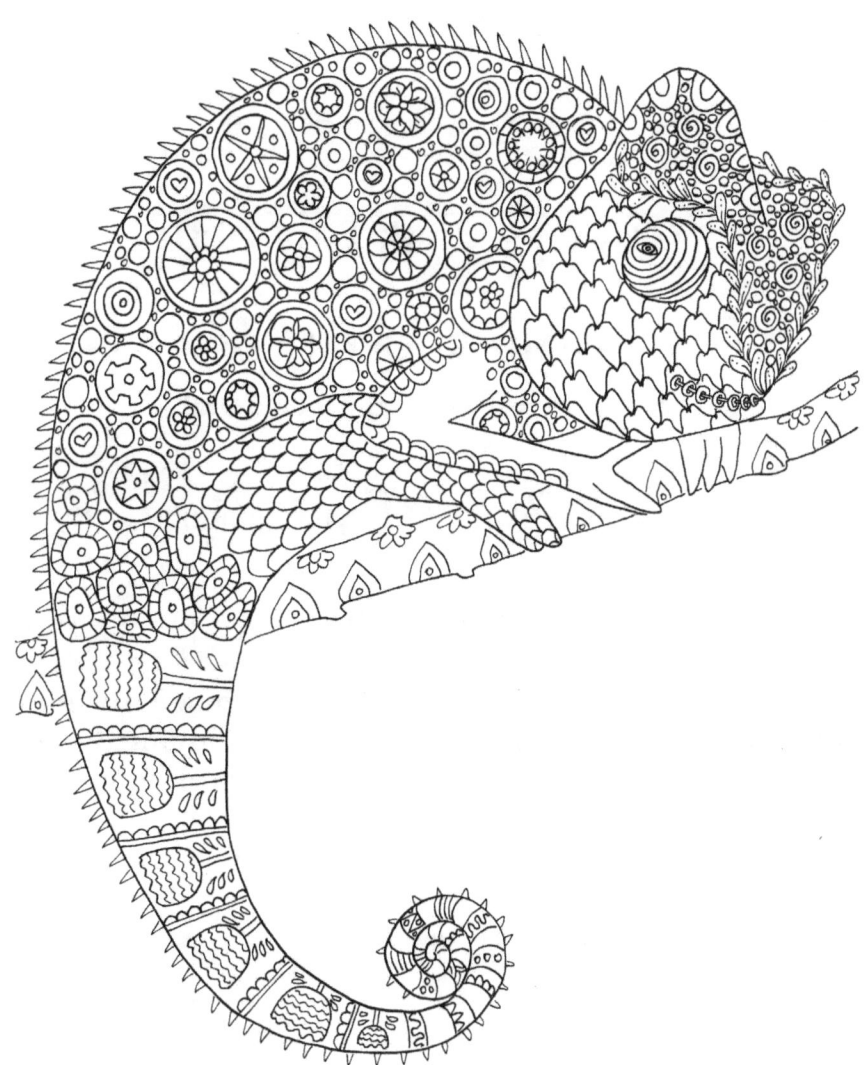

20 Pages of Stunning Animals to Color!

Coloring Book For Adults

DOODLE ANIMALS
Stress Relief Zentangle

Copyright © Maryna Salagub

First Edition

Distributed by: CreateSpace
ISBN-13: 978-1530261819
ISBN-10: 1530261813

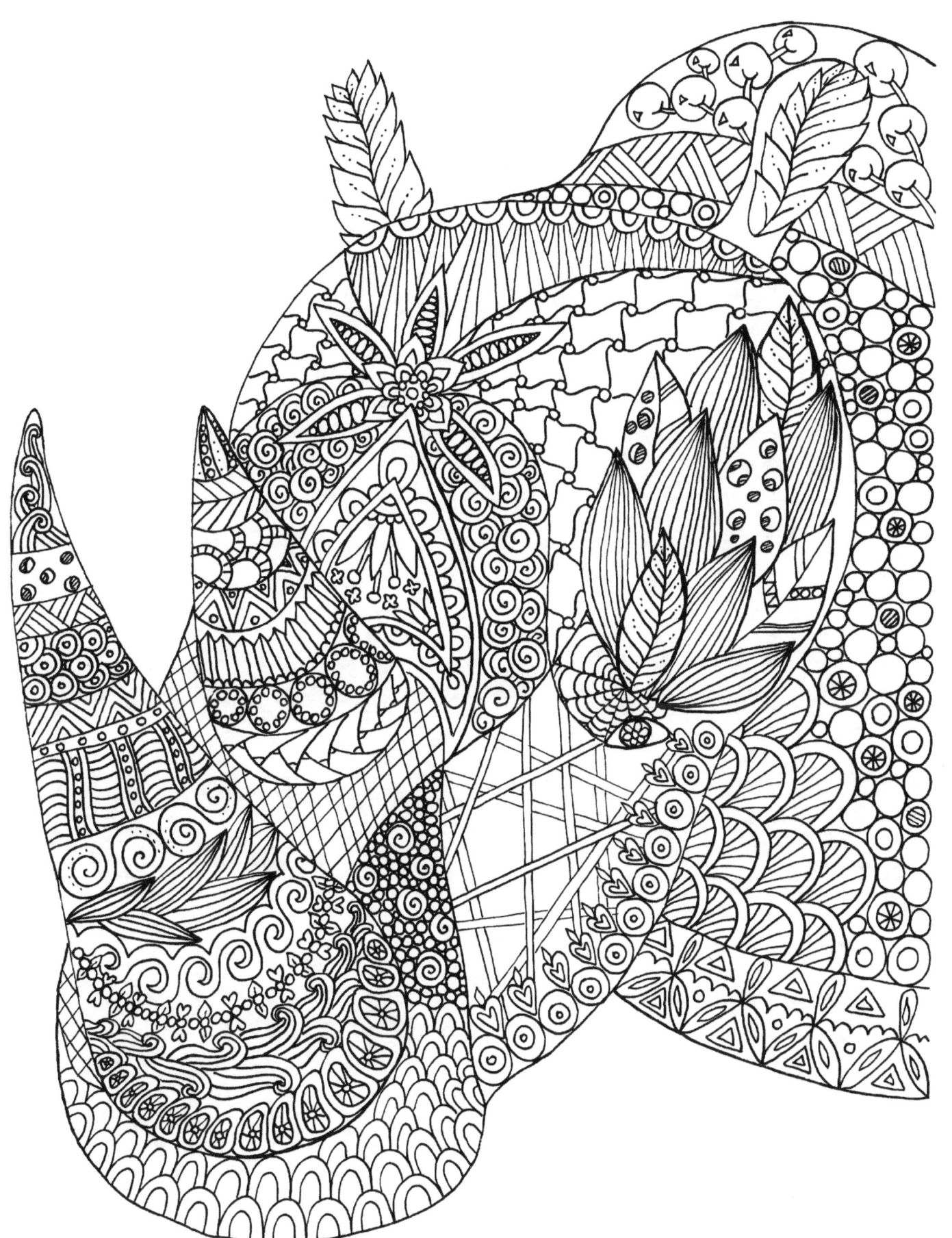

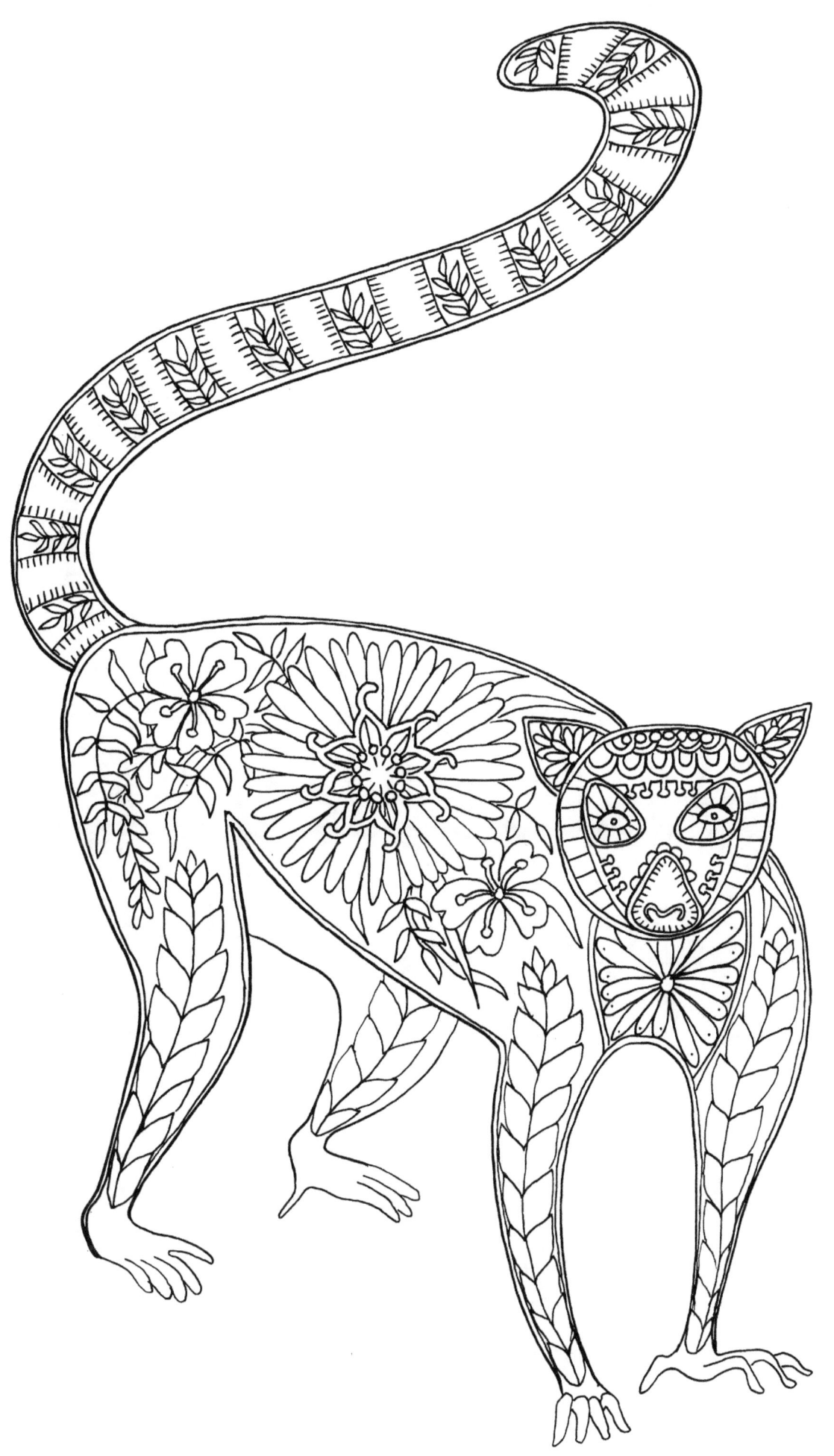

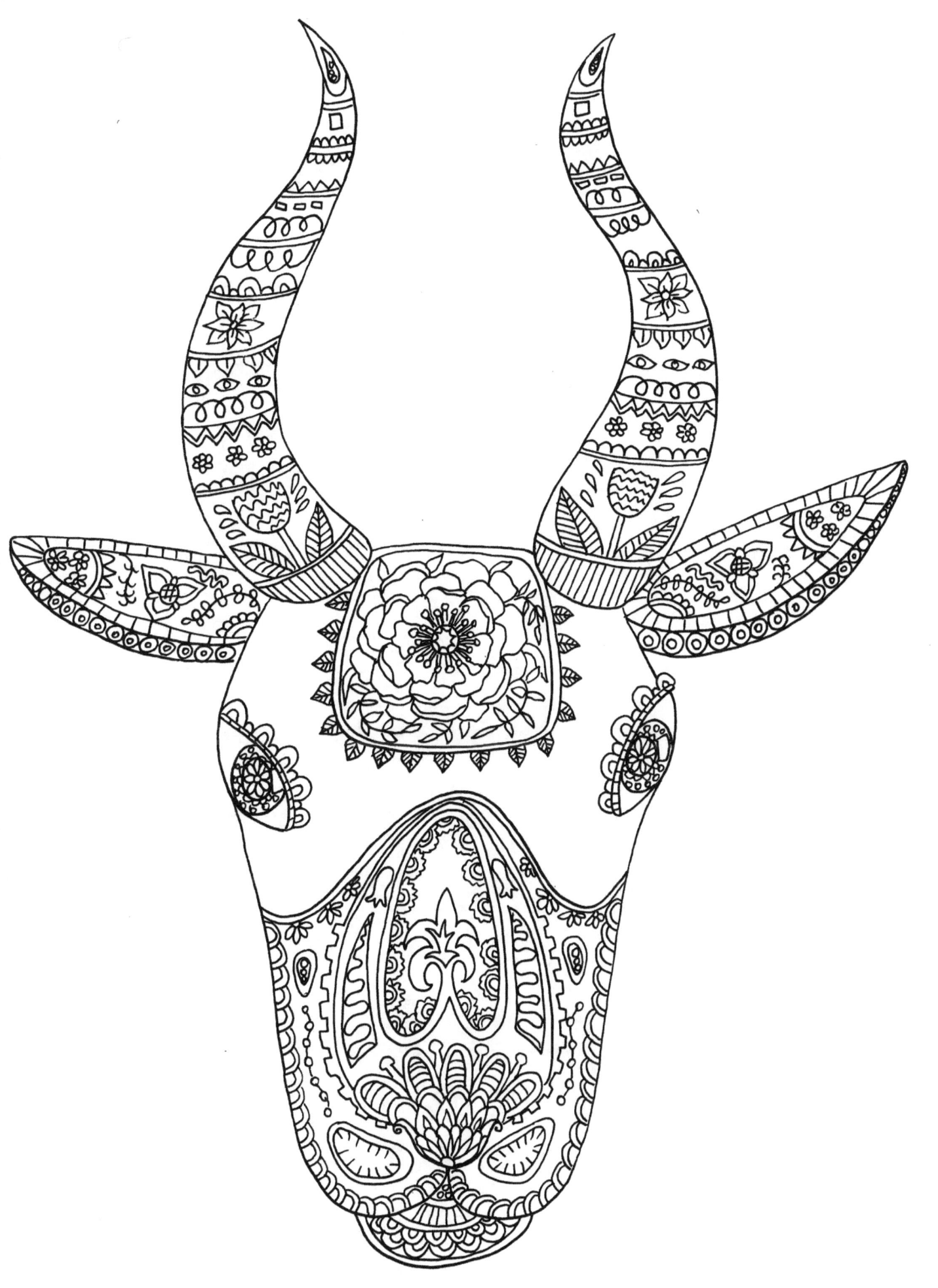

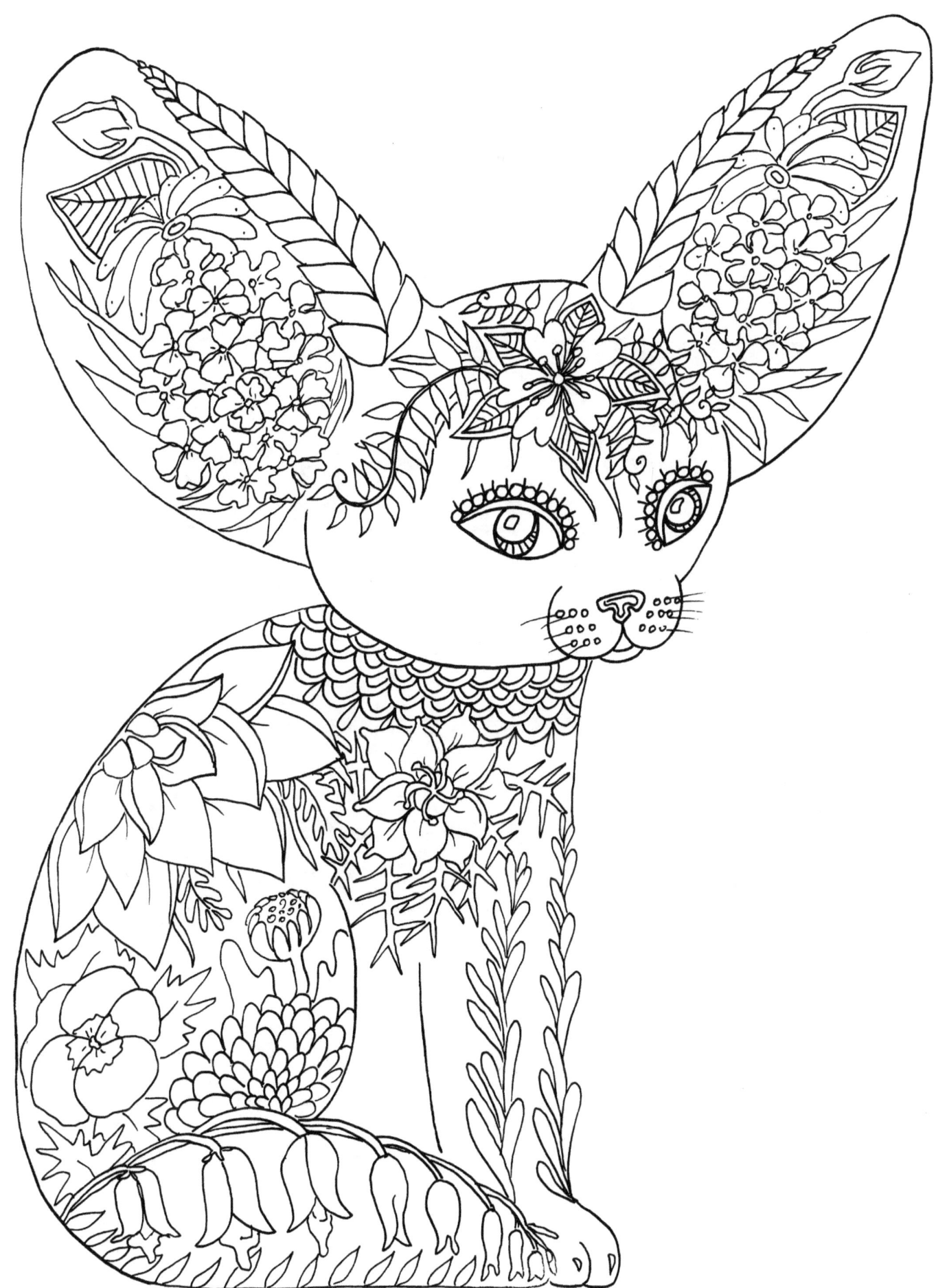

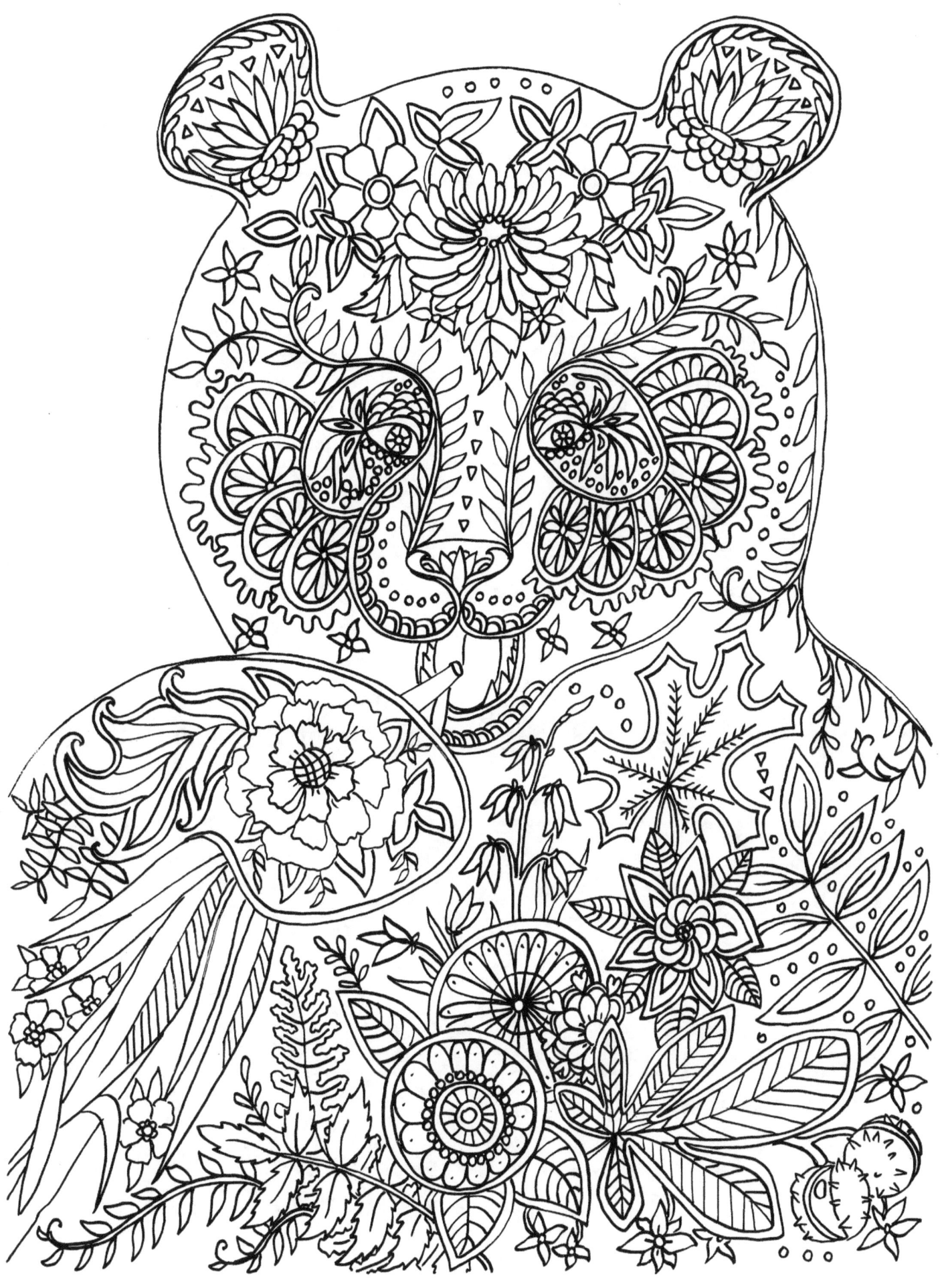

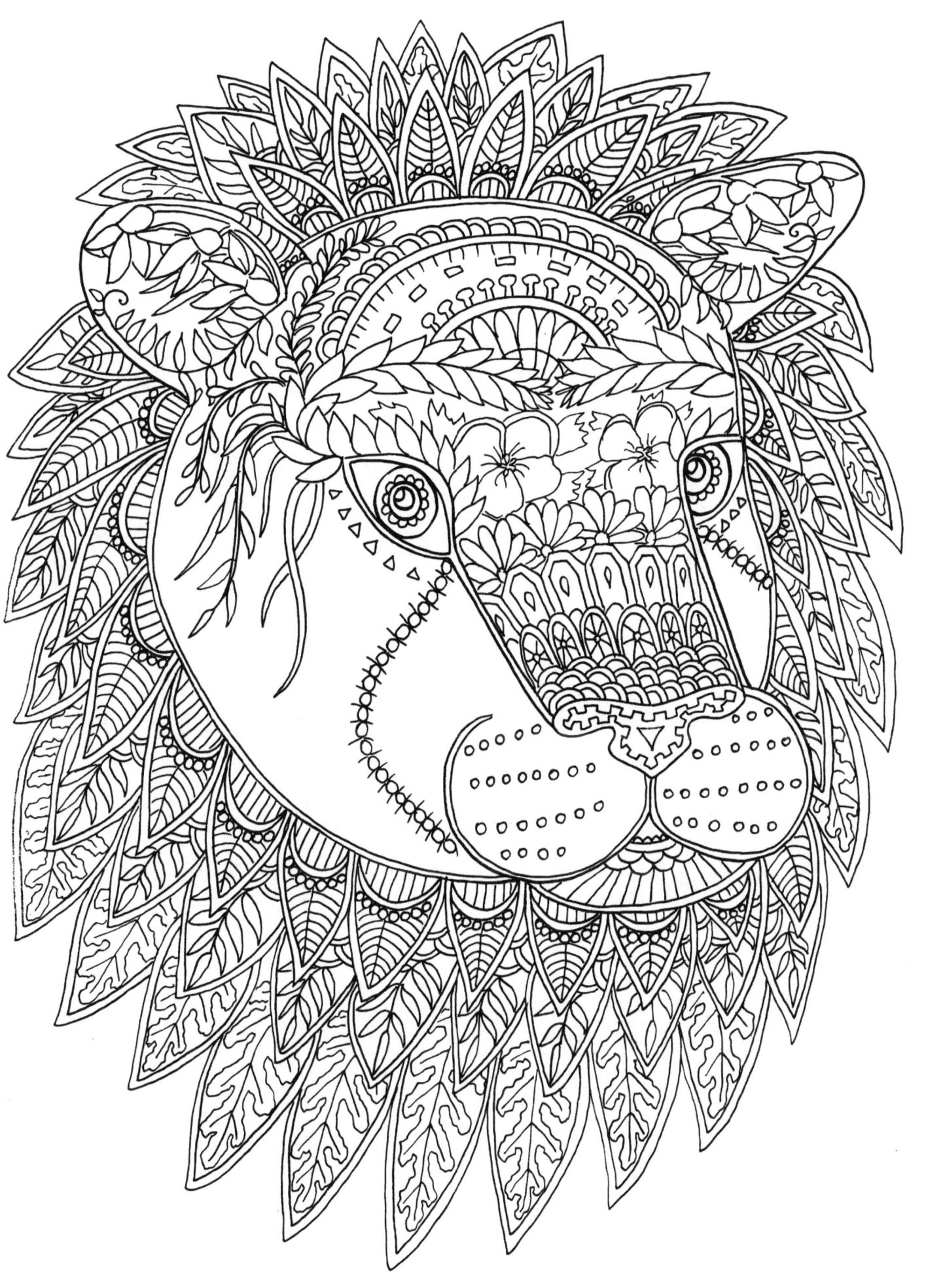

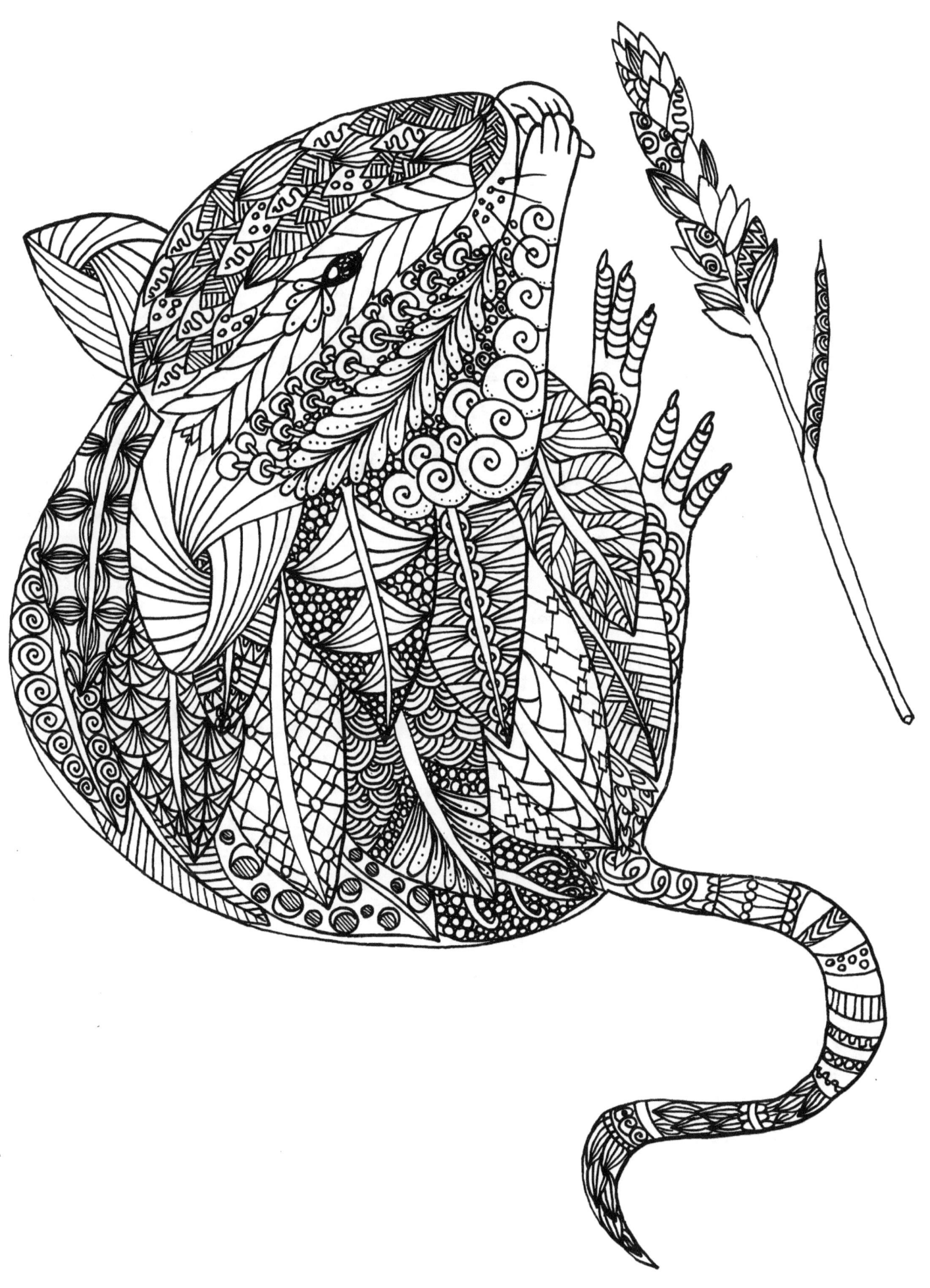

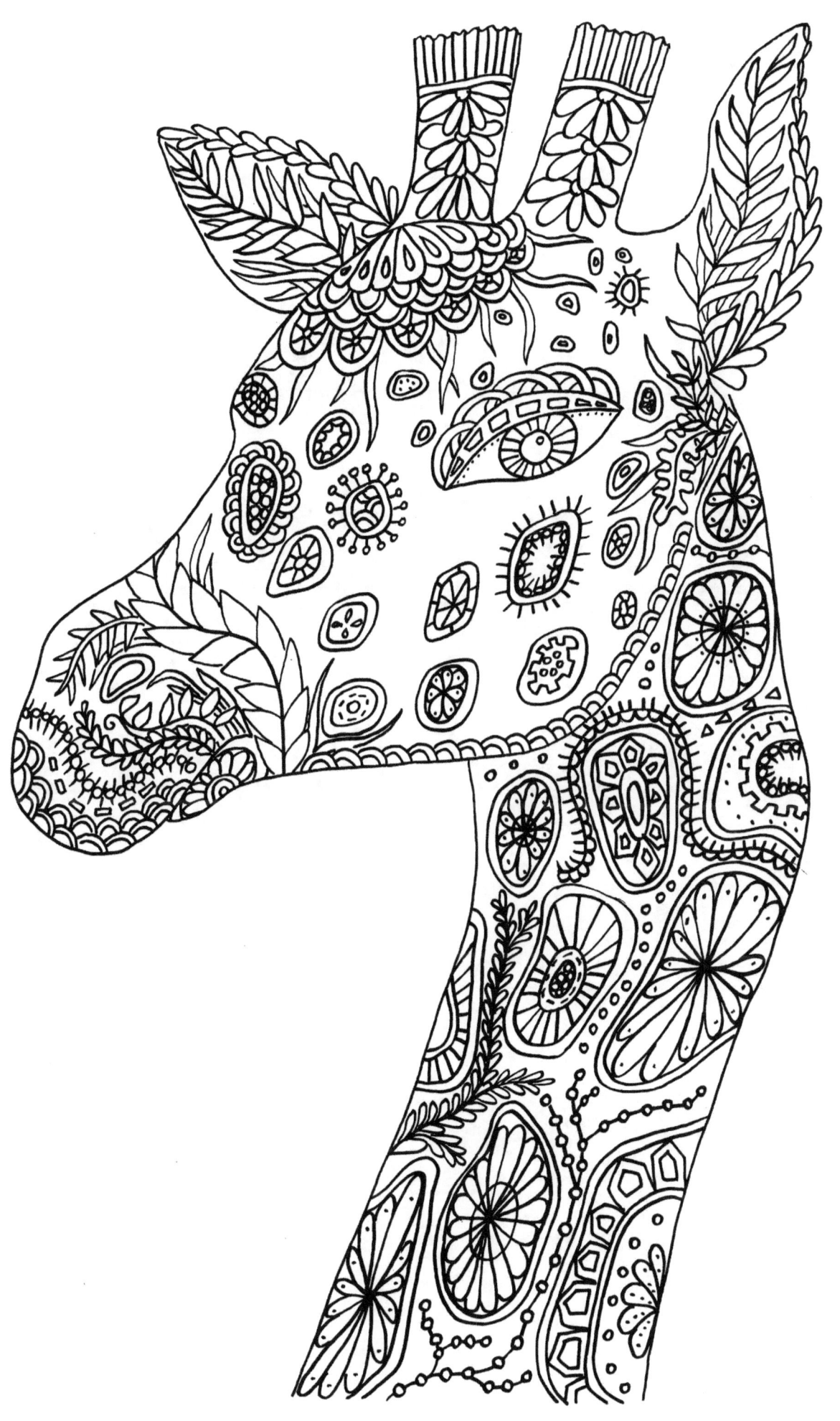

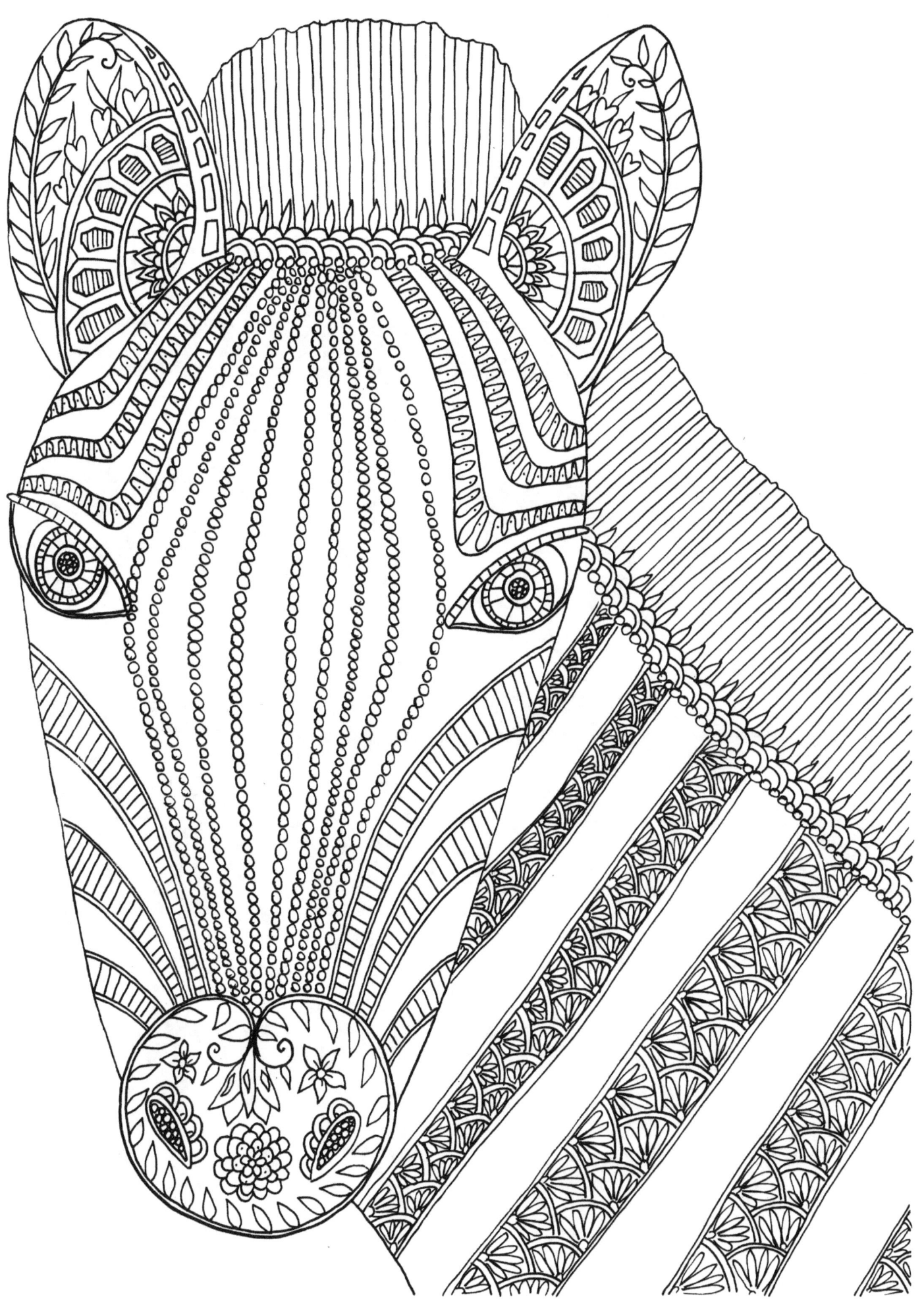

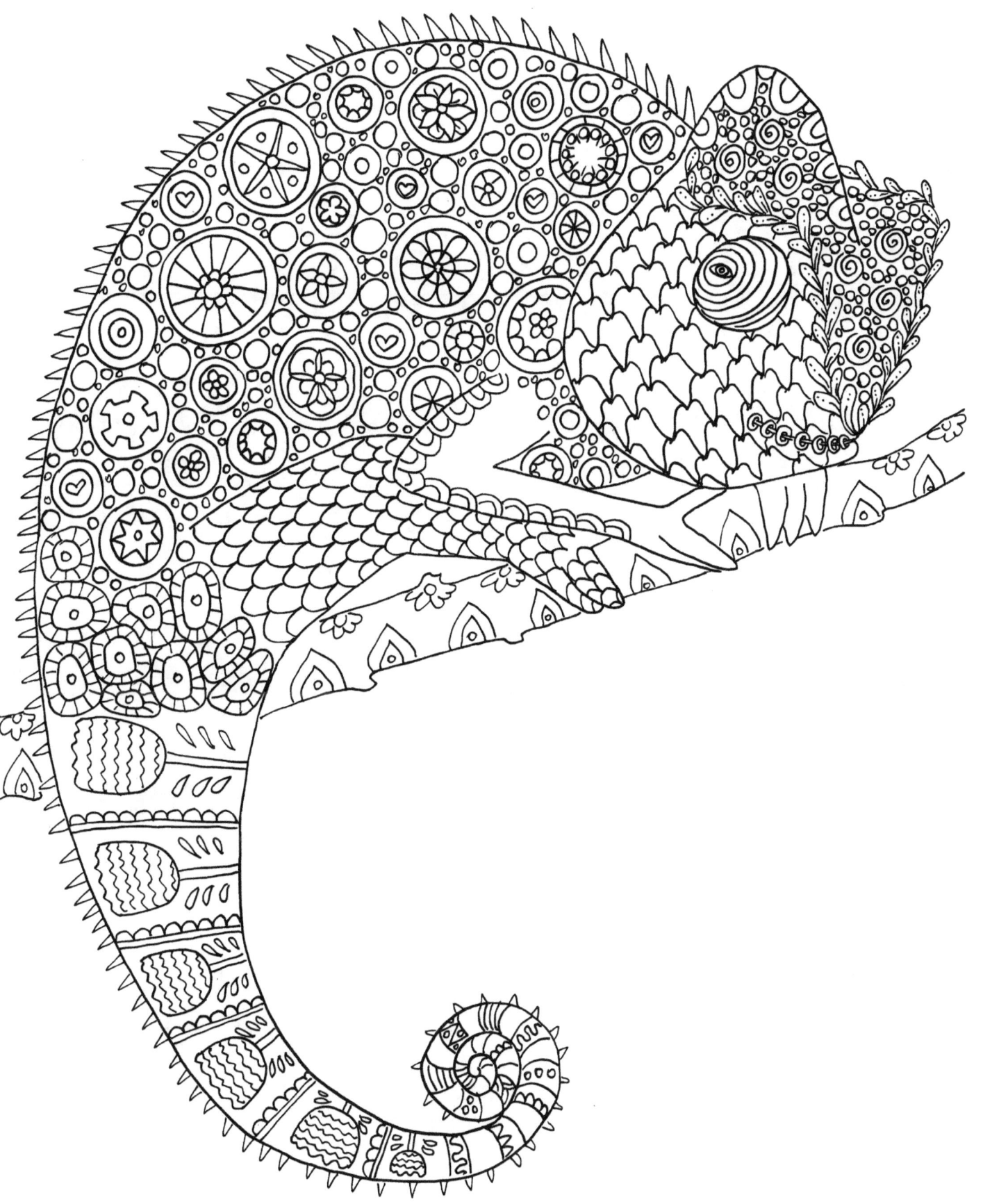

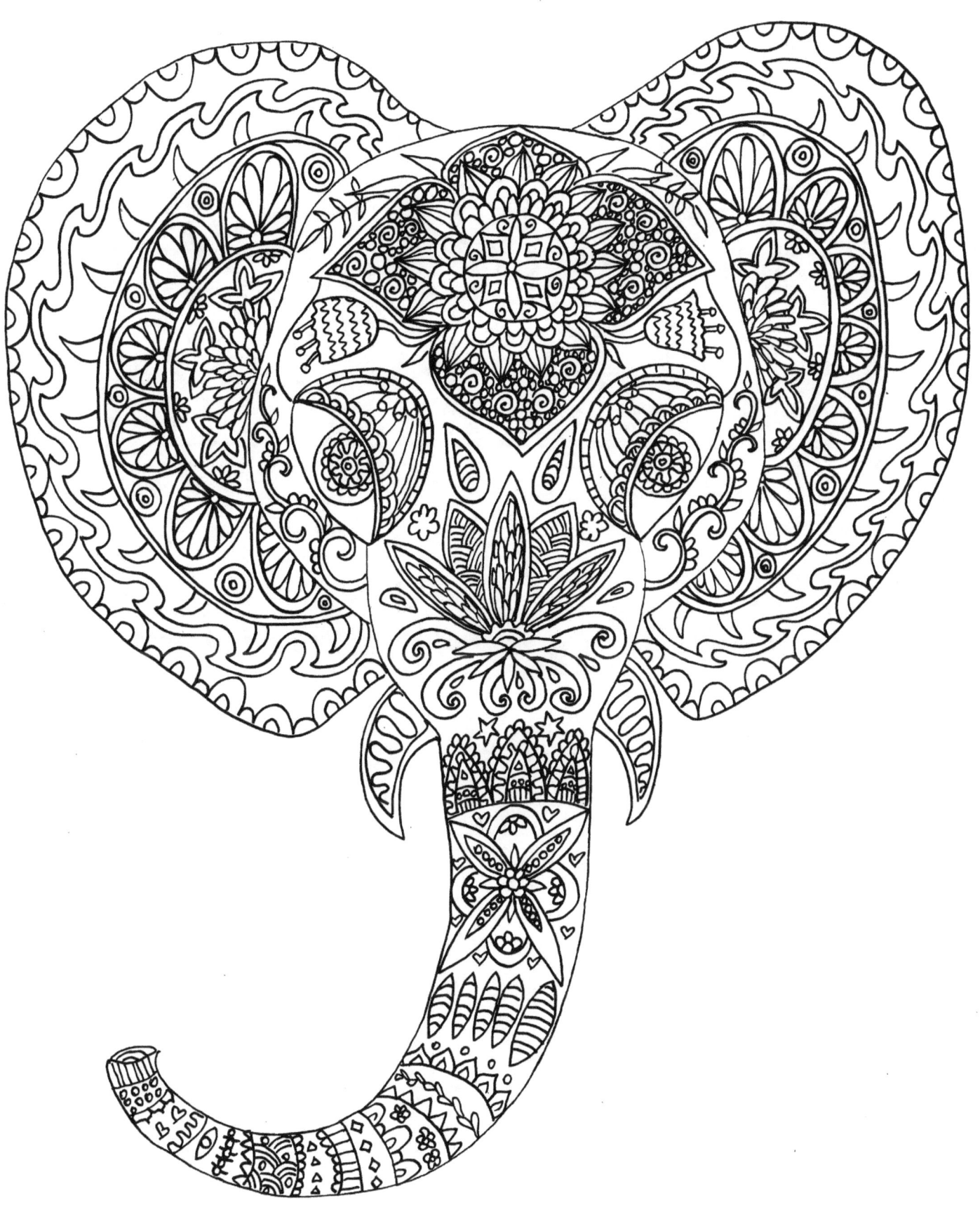

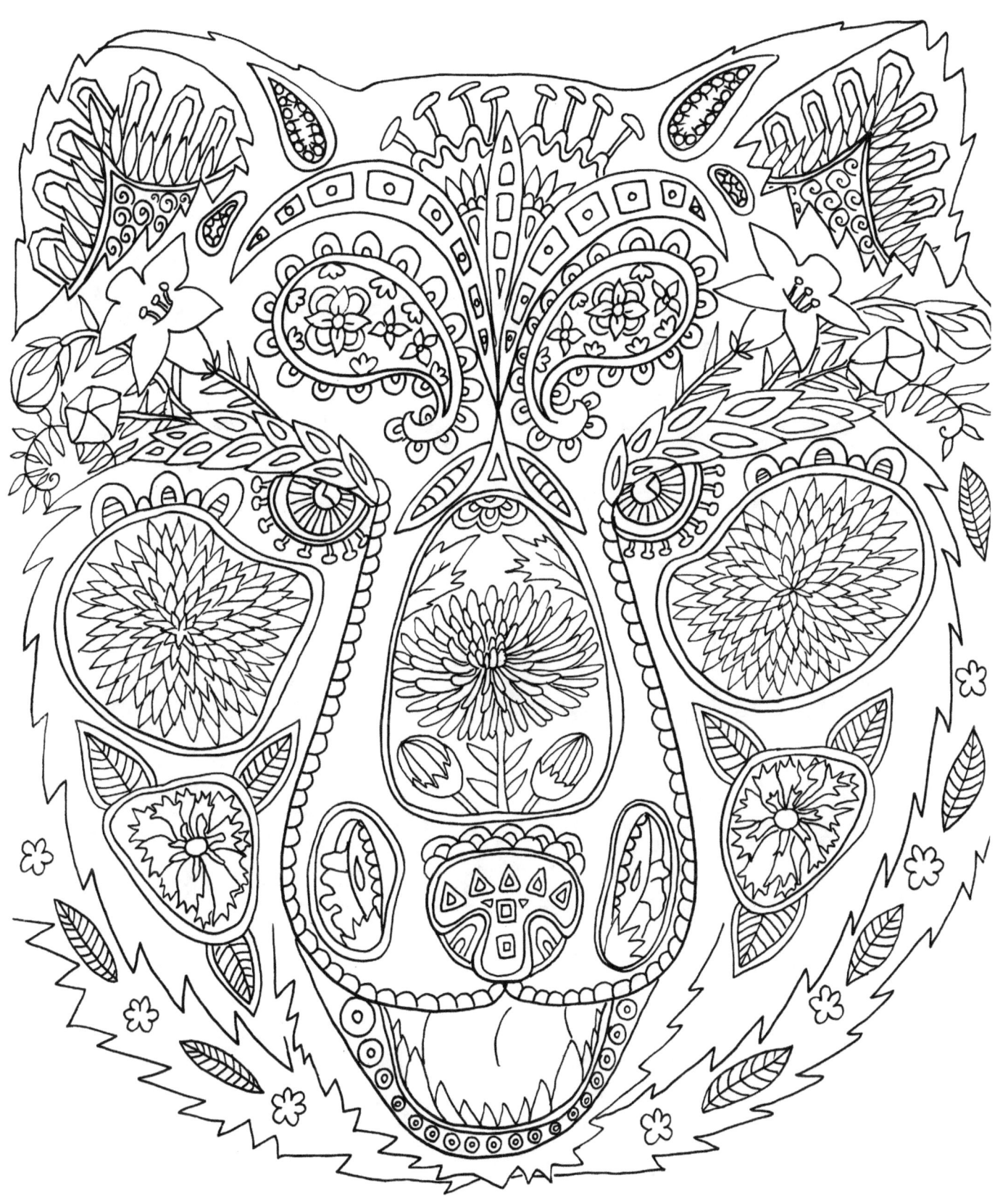

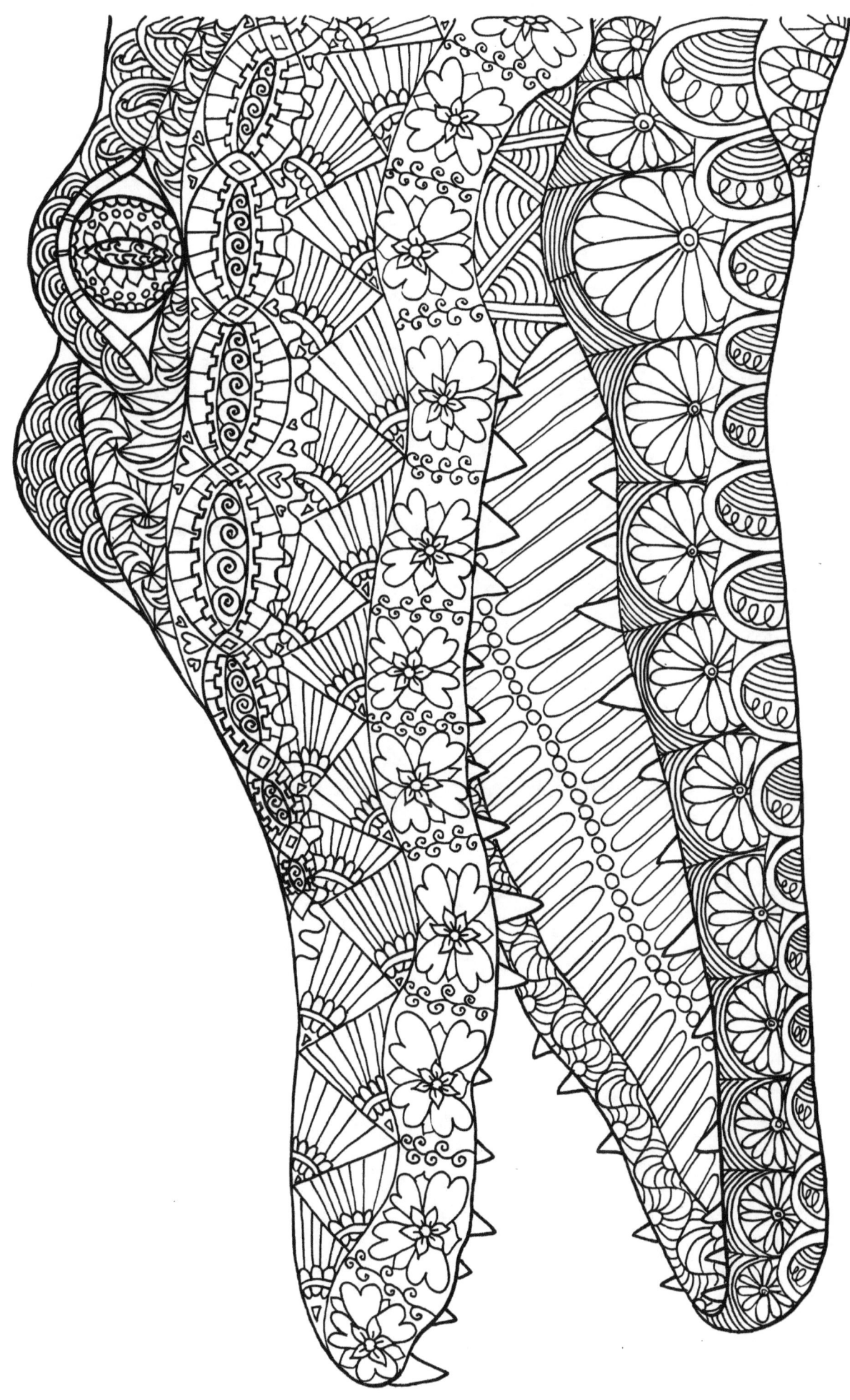

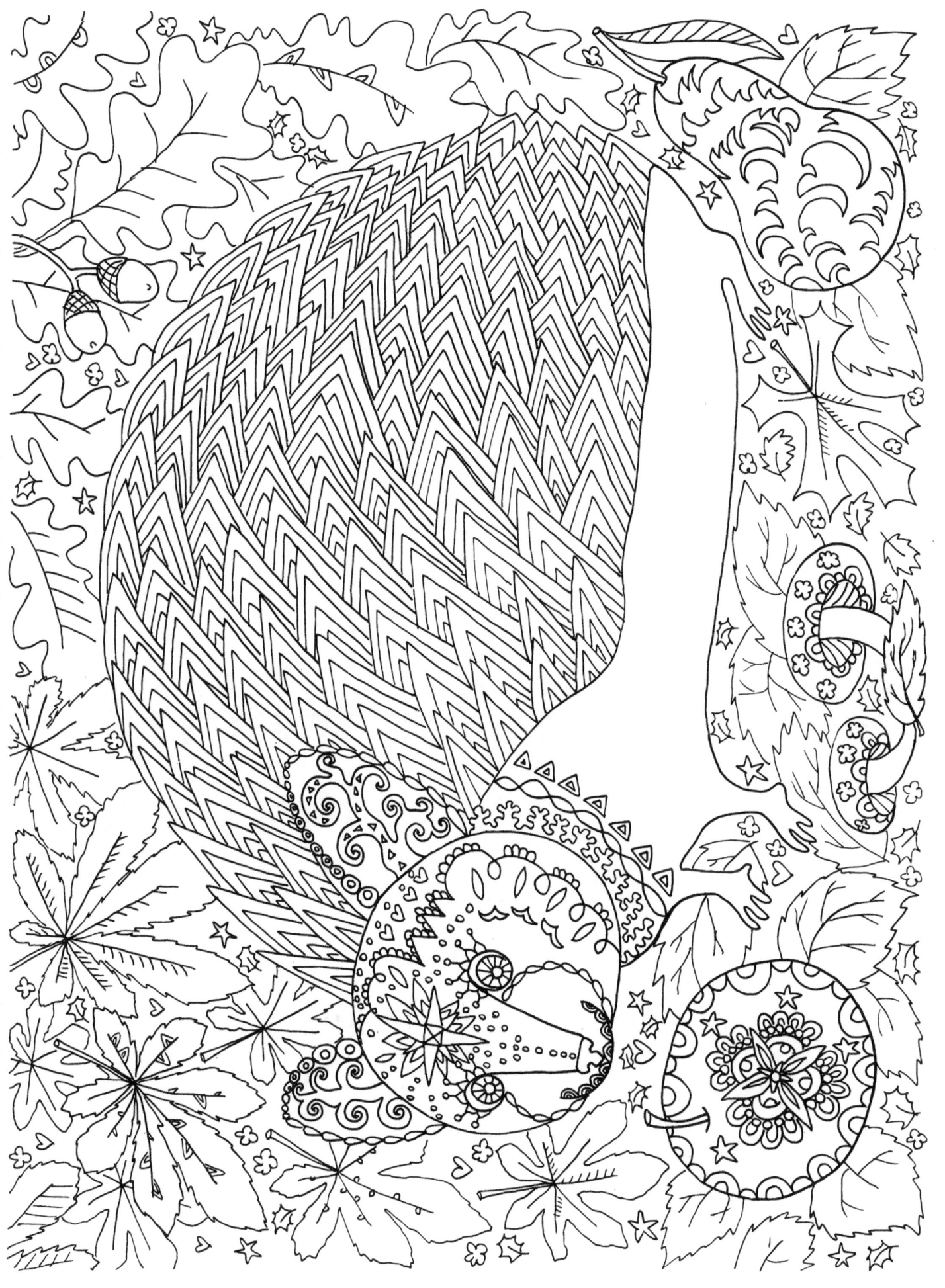

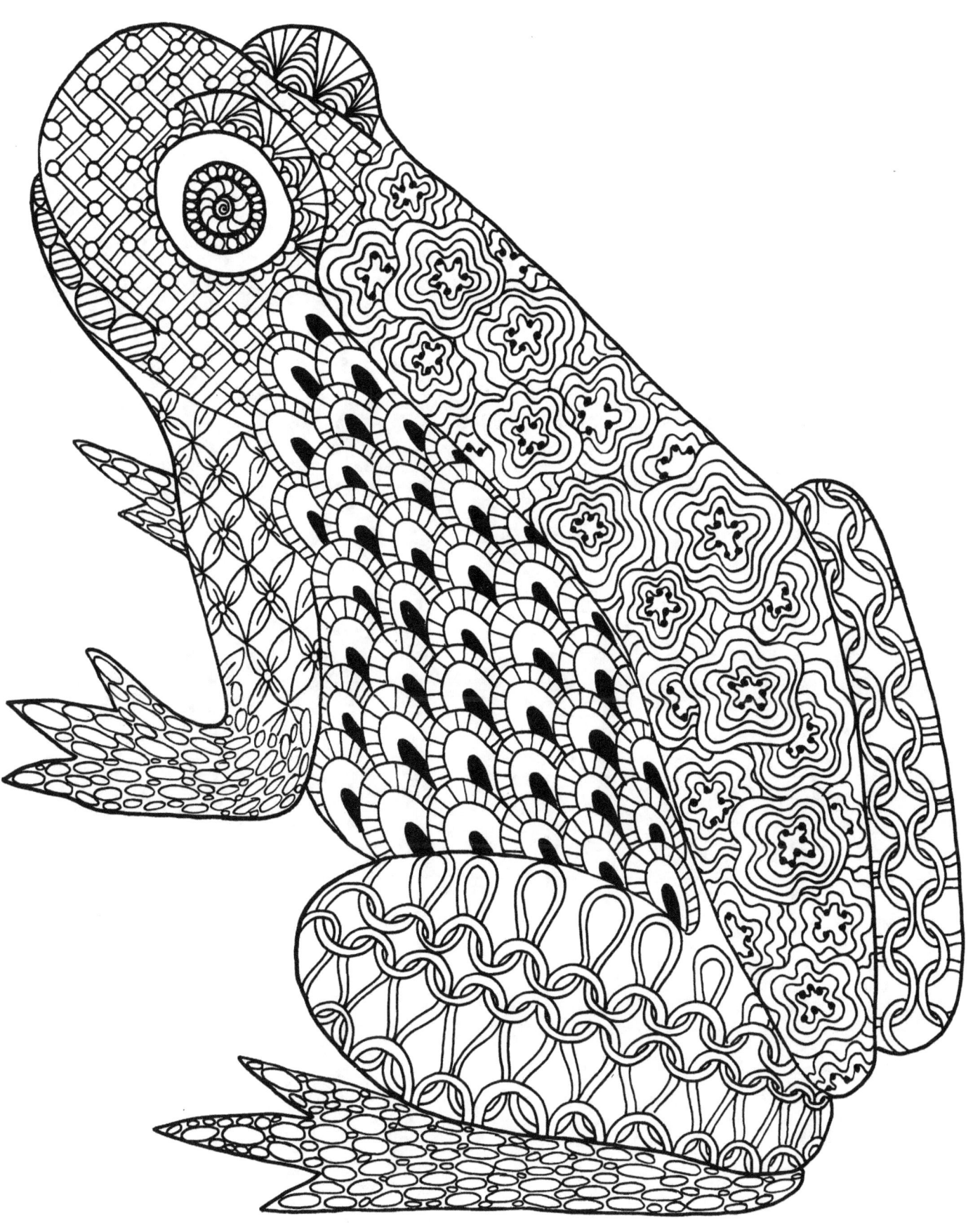

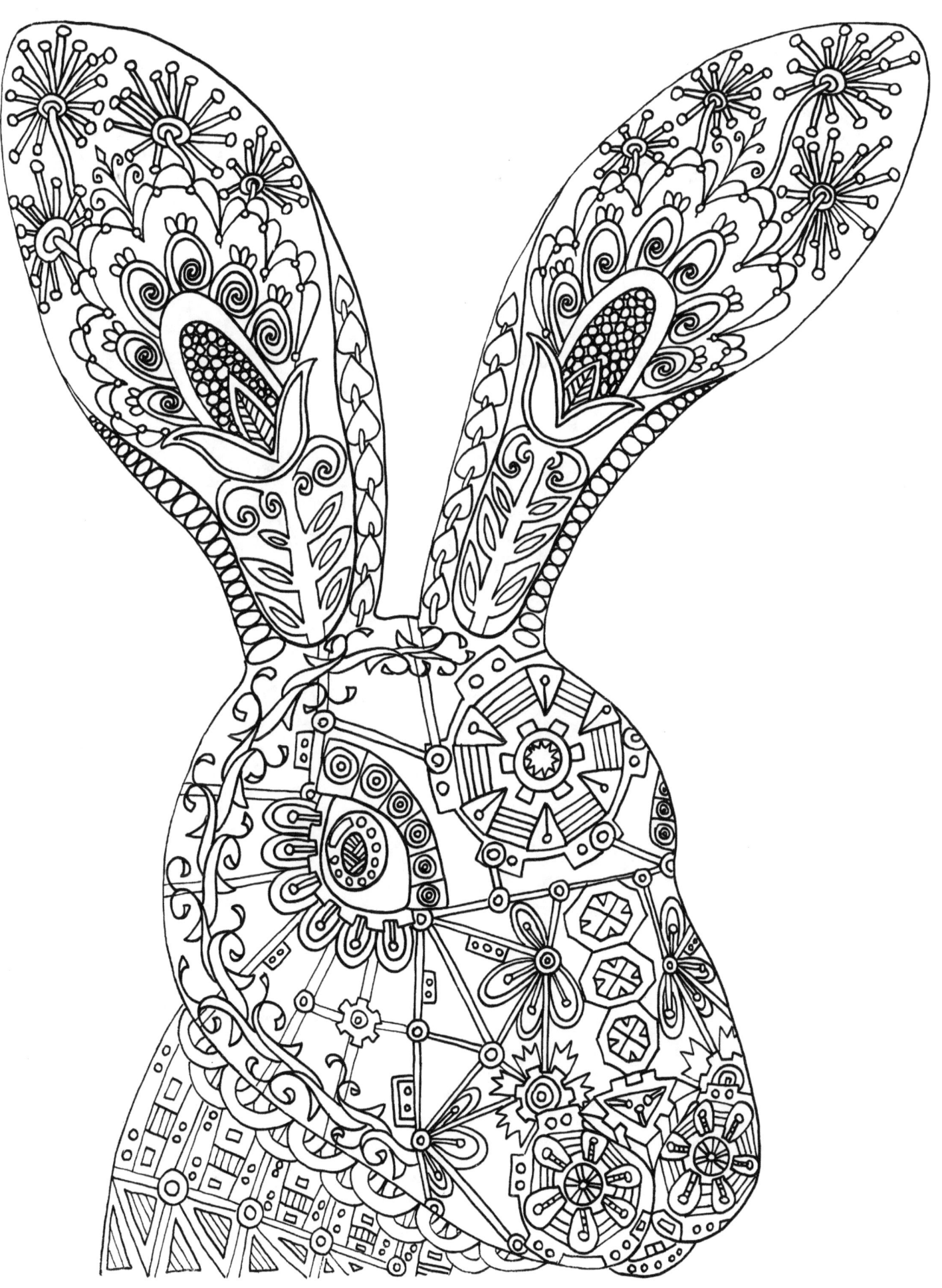

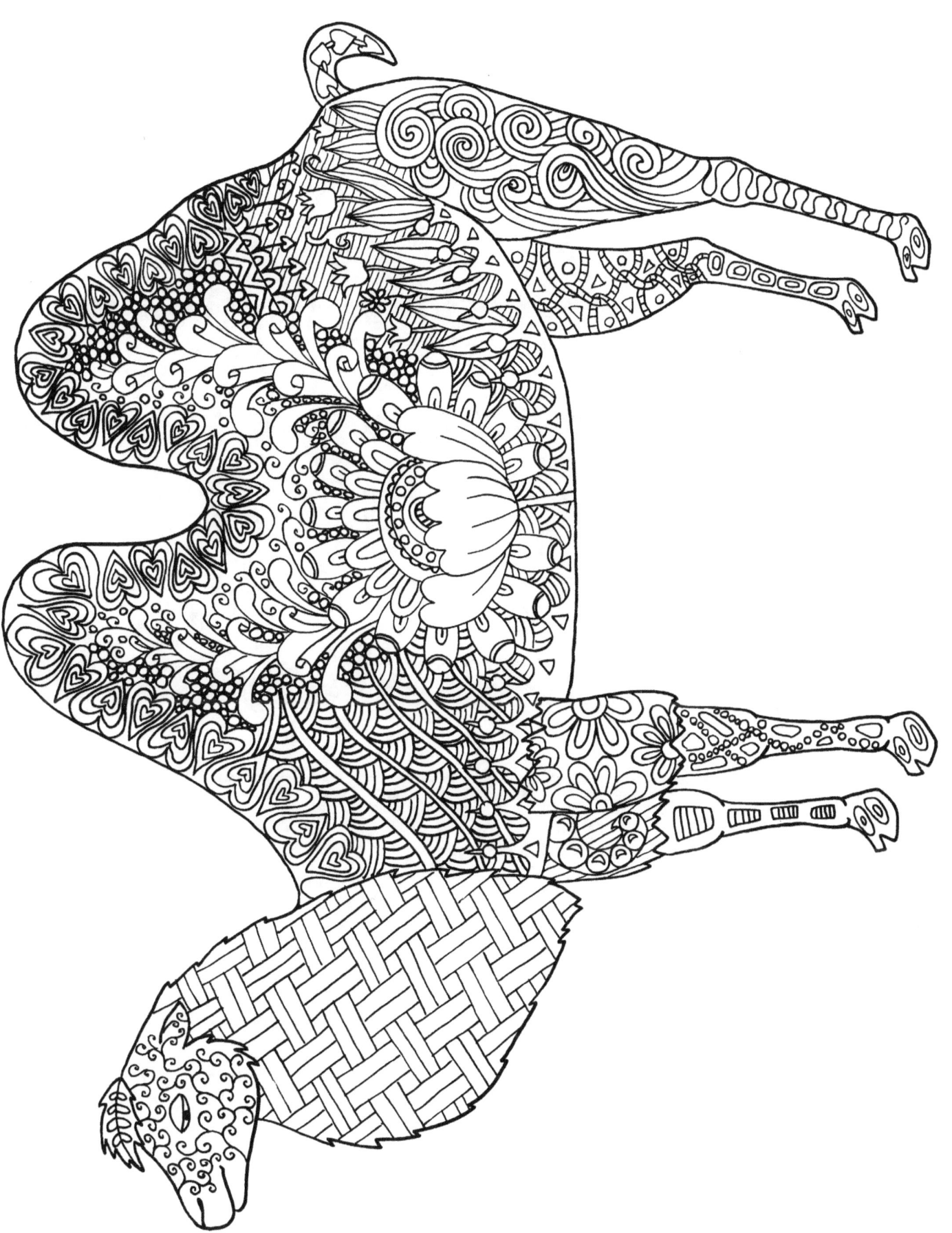

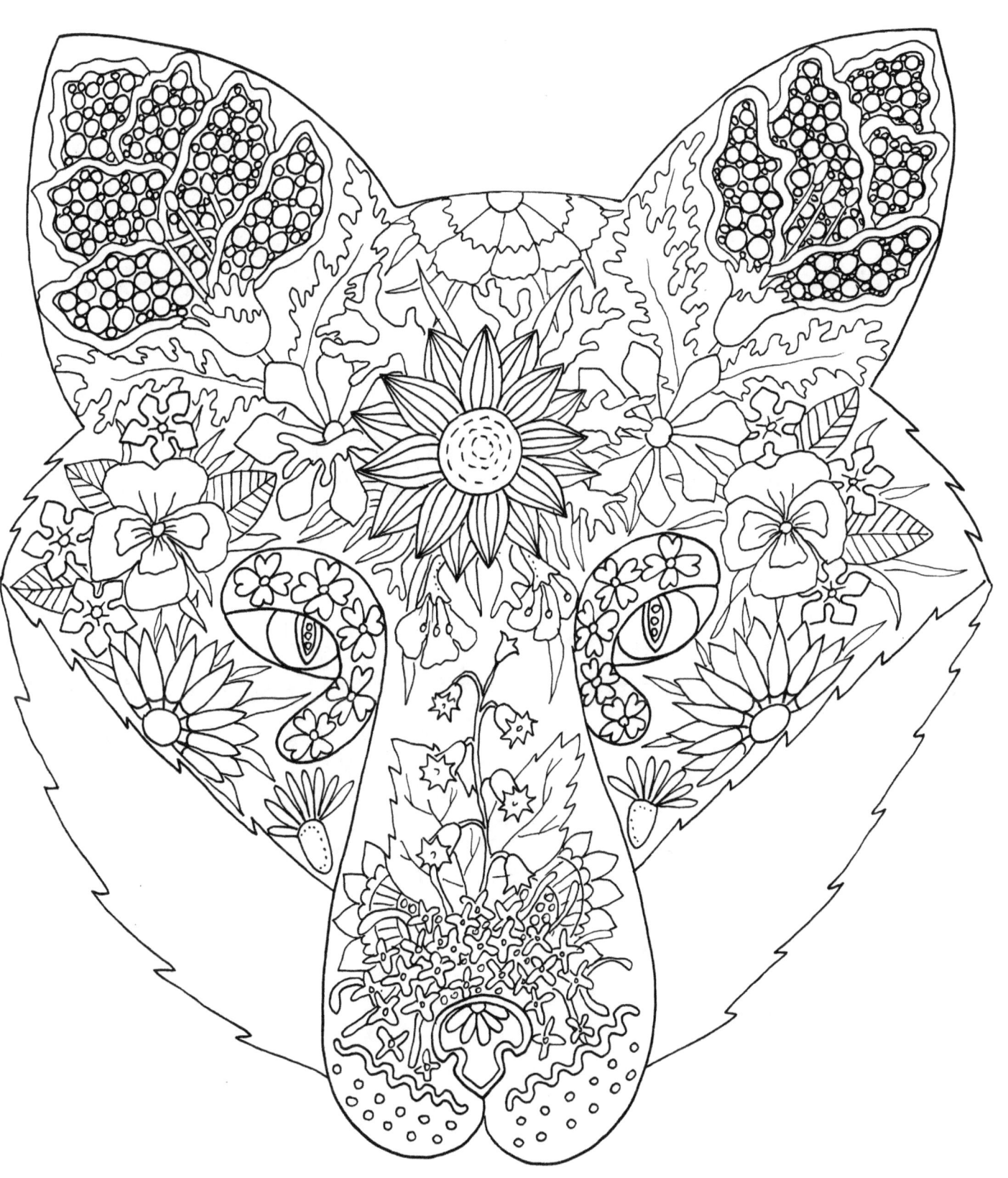

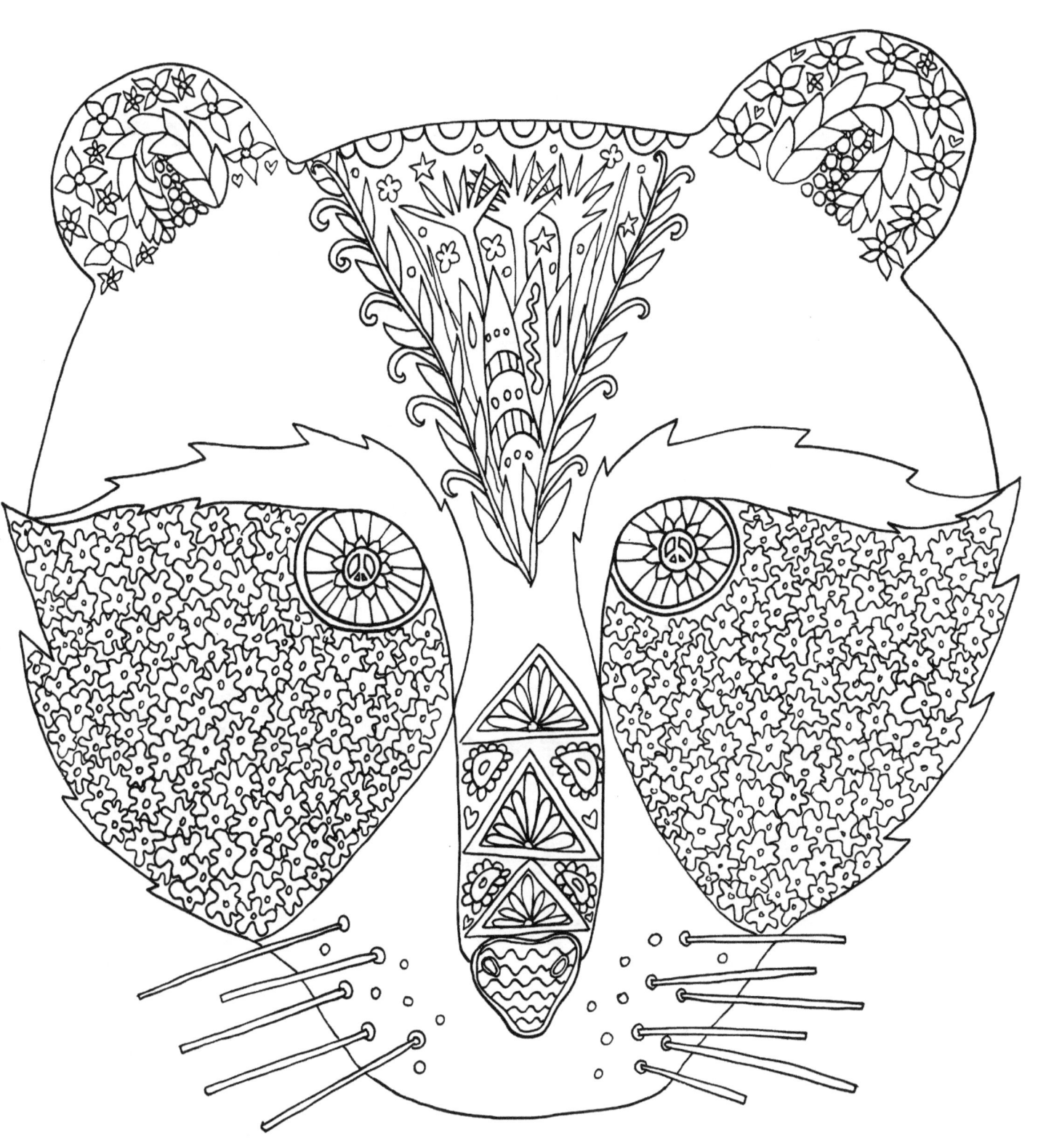

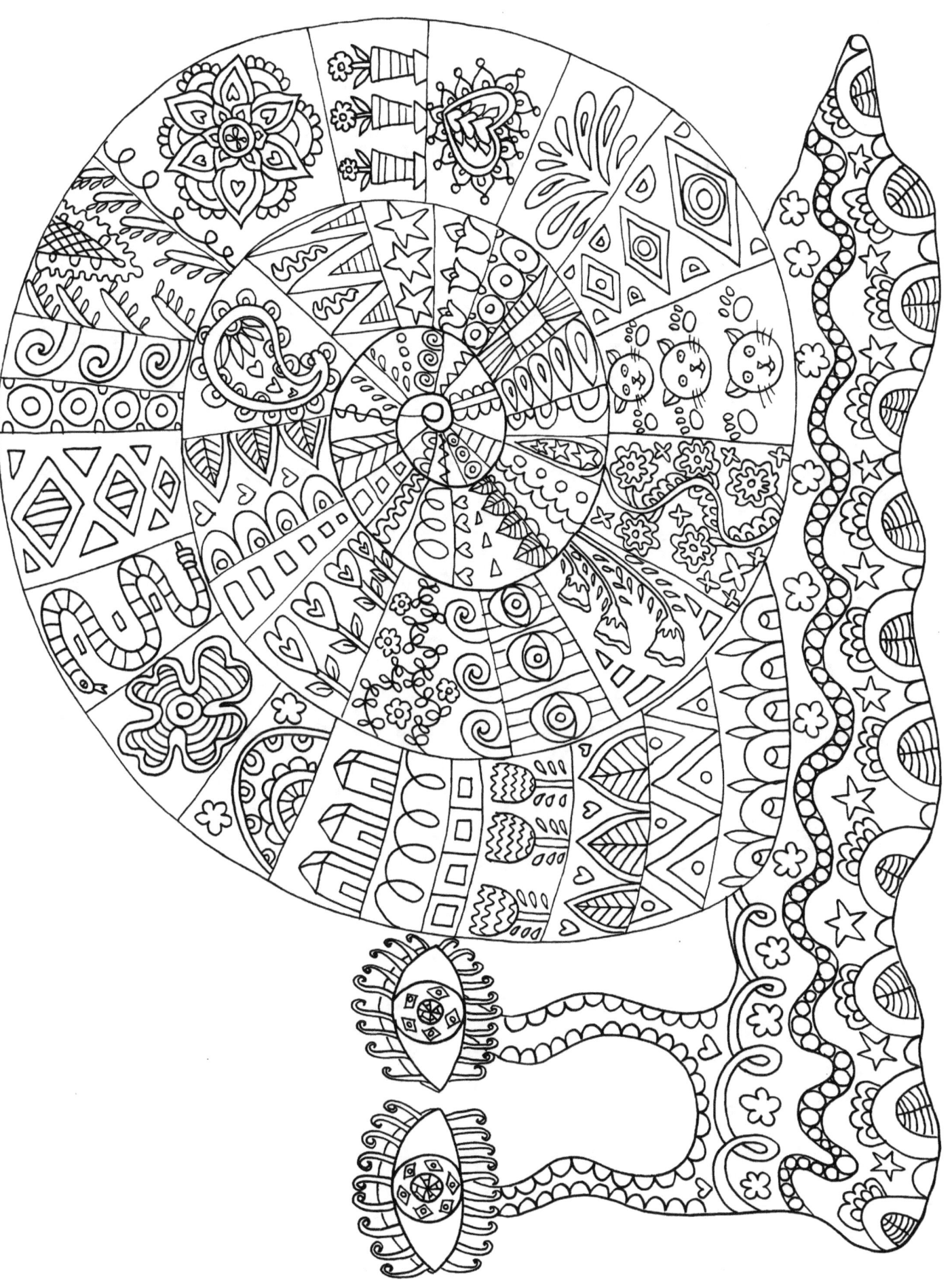

www.ingramcontent.com/pod-product-compliance
Lightning Source LLC
Chambersburg PA
CBHW080523190526
45169CB00008B/3028